THE DAY THE MOON SPLIT IN TWO

A GRIEF POETRY COLLECTION

BY TANZILA AHMED

DEDICATION

For Ammu

TABLE OF CONTENTS

SUDDEN DEATH

THE GARDEN SHE LOVED 10

MOON FACED 11

TRUST IN THE STORY 12

THE RITUALS OF DEATH 14

LET TIME STAND STILL 16

BILL OF DEATH 18

DUA 20

THE WET AND DRY LINE 21

GRAVEYARD

SCENTS OF JANNAH 24

SITTING GRAVESIDE 26

HABITUAL PATTERNS 27

HEADSTONE 28

JASMINES 29

TIME GOES FAST 30

JINN AT GRAVE 32

PATRIOTIC PUFF PIECE 33

TEARS BURIED IN THE GRAVEYARD OF MY CHEST 34

HAUNTING

IMPOSSIBLE EXISTENCE 36

PAST FOOTSTEPS FORWARD 37

ECHOES EXISTING 38

WHEN THE WIND RUSTLES 39

LAST TOUCH: FIRST TOUCH 40

CATARACT SURGERY 41

MY FACE IS HERS 42

COLD CREAM 43

ANNIVERSARY 44

MEMORIAL DAY 45

TRANSLATION TECHNOLOGY 46

THE PAGES OF HER SONG BOOK 47

WHO HOLDS THESE IMAGES 48

UNRAVELING 49

LONGING IN AEROGRAMS 51

SUNSETS 53

HEALING

MOTHER'S FALLOW GARDEN 56

SEVEN YEARS 57

CRY IF I WANT TO 58

PAPER THIN SKIN 59

DISPOSABLE FIRE 62

KHALA'S IFTAR 65

YOGURT CONTAINERS 66

ABBU TRIED 67

TIME PASS INTO THE PAST 68

GIGGLES AT GRAVES 69

PROLOGUE

On June 1, 2011 at 6 p.m., I got the message—while at my Oakland apartment—that my sisters were taking my mother to the hospital because she was sick. On June 2nd, at 1:35 a.m., she was pronounced dead. I caught the earliest flight to Southern California that I could get, but it was too late.

The following grief poems were written in the moments, the weeks, the months, the years after her passing.

Islamic mythology states that one of the signs of the coming of the end of the world is the moon splitting in two. The day Ammu died, the moon split in two.

SUDDEN DEATH

CHAPTER 1

إِنَّا للهِ وَإِنَّا إِلَيْهِ رَاجِعُونَ

Inna lillahi wa inna ilayhi raji'un

Indeed, to Allah we belong and to Him we return.

THE GARDEN SHE LOVED

It was her garden that killed her eventually —
not toxic shrubs, or poison leaves
not a thorn or ivy —
just an infection on her leg
that festered
after a day of gardening
amongst the plants
she loved.

MOON FACED

My mother's face used to remind me of the moon
round and fair
the acne pockmarks like the cratered surface
cheek dimples like meteor shadows.

She was plump
a celestial body to reckon with
with gravity so powerful it could make waves.

Her face looked like a 12th century Persian painting
a Rumi poem embodied
or maybe, moon paintings and lunar poems
just remind me of my mother.

The moon face
with the almond shaped eyes and thick arched eyebrows
upturned chin and pursed red lips
stare back from the ancient gilded parchment
like the moon had never set.

On her wedding day
my father looked through a handheld mirror
to gaze upon her face for the first time
their eyes met
someone asked what he saw
and he said a beautiful moon.

On the day she died
the moon split in two
and the world came to an end.

We've been struggling to piece
the moon back together ever since.

TRUST IN THE STORY

لَا يُكَلِّفُ اللَّهُ نَفْسًا إِلَّا وُسْعَهَا

Allah does not burden a soul beyond what it can bear. (Quran 2:286)

Is this life cycle on recycle
cycling a legacy
a repeat of legendary?
How much more can I handle
of this fated tale?
What if survival to normal
is just a story of survival?
What if there is no happy ending —
just a struggle for perpetual?

They say the Ultimate Storyteller
only tells tales
that the heroine can handle —
but what if she can't?
Did Ammu's death come
because she could handle her tale no more?

The body should be laid out, stripped of its garments and its joints loosened, if possible. A cloth should be placed over the private parts, between the navel and the knees so that the washers do not look at the pubic area of the dead person. The stomach should be pressed to expel any remaining impurities.

A rag or cloth should be used to wash the body and the washing should begin with the places on the right side of the body washed during wudhu.

After completing the wudhu, the woman's hair should be undone if it was braided and the hair thoroughly washed. Then the rest of the body should be washed, turning the body on its side so as to complete the right side before washing the left.

The body should be washed a minimum of three times and the water should have some cleaning agent in it, like soap or disinfectant. The final washing should have some perfume in it, such as camphor or the like.

The body should then be dried and the hair combed out.

Source: 'Funerals According to the Quran and Sunnah,'
sunnahonline.com

THE RITUALS OF DEATH

He whispered sweet suras
bending down near Ammu's face.
She was wrapped in white
with just her face showing
framed by her white cotton hijab
I had tied tight
tucking in her stray hairs just so —
the hair I had tenderly washed and dried
in the sterile room with that strong camphor smell
tears streaming down - so many tears -
I had to dry her hair all over again.

Her head had felt so heavy. So full of gravity.

I sat in the folding chair placed nearest her head
the table that strapped her in a cage
sitting vigil until she was to be wheeled away
to the Salat-al-Janazah and then
the grave.

Abbu bent down near her head.
I peeked up from between
my tears, my dupatta, my downturned face
wanting to give him a moment
but wanting to see what he would do.
He was wearing a white kurta and on his head a white thopi –
I wondered numbly who dressed him that morning
how he knew what to wear.
His dark skin was heavy with wrinkles
his eyes were sunken in
he had aged overnight
he had no tears in his eyes.
He seemed
devoid of emotions.
He didn't look at us
his daughters.

He waved his hand in front of his face
and close to her face
like he was trying to will her to breathe in the whispered Arabic words.
What was she thinking? Was she recoiling?
Like she would have if she were alive?

What was this ritual?
Who would teach me these things now that she was gone?
Who would I ask now?

When I was born, it must have looked like this too.
It was Abbu who had whispered into my ear
The first words I've ever to hear – *Allahu Akbar* –
The azaan, the call to prayer.

Who taught him to do that? This ritual?
My newlywed parents eleven months into their marriage
 with a newborn in their arms.
Telegrams and aerograms barely closing the gap
between half the world and their home.

Here we are thirty years later.
In birth and death
first words and last words.
Abbu whispered suras

he walked out of the room,
barely acknowledging the presence of daughters
holding vigil by his wife's side
he didn't even see us
but for me
it was like it was the first time I saw him.

Azaan crescendo-ed loud from the electronic speakers of the minaret
my heart sank and I stood up.
Tenderly I performed the ritual of placing
the right cloth over her face
and then the left cloth
and tied it closed.
It was time.

Let Time Stand Still

Pause // Stop // Wait
This can't be my truth, can it?

... *Take it back!* I sob into the phone. *Take it back!*

Wandering lost and aimless
in the home I grew up in
mind like a sieve
unable to latch onto much of anything.

... *Take it back! You didn't mean it! She's fine!*

In this time pass
time stands still in perpetuity
denial of time from doing what it does best —
ticking forward.

... *She was just sick! The doctors are going to fix her! TAKE IT BACK...*

Life spins around me
but I can't seem to catch onto it
lost in myself
I pause, not knowing what I started
I start, not remembering why.

... *Please, take it back. This can't be real. Pleasepleaseplease take it back....*

My truth has changed
the ultimate universal paradigm shift
an explosion so big
the world's axis tilted
just a bit.

... *Take it back....* I cry into the phone, even after I hear her hang up.

Minutes pass // Hours pass // Days pass

Months pass
YEARS
Time stands still

Pause // Stop // Wait
Let it be still for only a moment

... I sob into dial tone, screaming at an empty phone.

Bill Of Death

The co-pay for my mother's death was $100.
Isn't that the damnedest thing?

The bill arrived on one crisp white page, folded with precision. Envelope enclosed. Medical insignia gracing the header. Rip away bill on the footer.

The paper graced the magnetic bulletin board with all the rest of Ammu's bills. She was terrible at finances. The bulletin board was littered with her bills, all asking for her "estate" to pay her debt back. Her estate, we scoffed. We would find unopened envelopes stashed like Easter eggs hidden around the house in plastic grocery bags. We found them for months after she died, well after we thought we had sorted the finances away.

The medical bill for her death stayed on that wall for months, none of sure why we needed to pay a fee for the hospital service that killed our mother. They killed her, you know. They misdiagnosed her, mistreated her until her body gave up on her. Undiagnosed blood infection. That's what her death certificate says.

It was paid, eventually.
We were tired of the reminder of her death on our wall.
But to have to pay a $100 for her death?
It's the damnedest thing, really.

[ritual]

The angels fly near when someone dies to guide the soul to their grave. Say ameen, for the chance that you say it at the same time as an angel says it. If you say ameen at the same time, all your sins will be forgiven. So say ameen.

Source: Muslim lady at the mosque

DUA

Say Ameen —
    and wish for the chance of an angel's synchronized breath.

Say Ameen —
    hope for nur to fill ruh when the angels come to her death.

Say Ameen —
    may all of my prayers bring her soul peace and rest.

Say Ameen —
    may angels guide her to jannah to fill her with bliss.

        Ameen.

THE WET AND DRY LINE

But
where
is the line
between where
rain and sunlight
exists?
Where is
the boundary
the point
the pivot
where water ends
air begins
where wet cement
turns
dry?

GRAVEYARD

CHAPTER 2

السَّلَامُ عَلَيْكُمْ أَهْلَ الدِّيَارِ مِنَ الْمُؤْمِنِينَ وَالْمُسْلِمِينَ ، وَإِنَّا إِنْ
شَاءَ اللهُ بِكُمْ لَلَاحِقُونَ ، نَسْأَلُ اللهَ لَنَا وَلَكُمُ الْعَافِيَةَ

As-salaamu 'alaykum ahl-ad-diyaari mi-nal-mu'mineena
wal-muslimeena, wa in-naa in shaa'-allaahu la-
laaḥiqoona, nas'al-ullaaha lanaa wa-lakumul-'aafiya

Peace be upon you all, inhabitants of the dwellings
amongst the believers and the Muslims. Indeed, we are,
Allah willing, soon to follow, we ask Allah for wellbeing
for us and for you.

Scents Of Jannah

The earthy smell
of stained henna hands
mingles with the dirt
from the grave.

Inhale deeply and
exhale tears
splashing into
dua extended palms.

Fresh flowers have life and therefore make tasbeeh and tahleel. Through this tasbeeh, reward is attained or punishment is decreased for any ordinary Muslim grave, and the visitors to a Mazaar gain a pleasant fragrance.

Therefore, placing them on any Muslim grave is allowed. Even if the deceased is experiencing punishment, through the blessings of the tasbeeh, it is lessened.

Source: 'Placing flowers and sheets and brightening the graves', islamieeducation.com

SITTING GRAVESIDE

I lay the purple iris down
after pulling at the dried weeds
kneel knees on the concrete wall outlining the grave.
I grab a clot of dirt
crumbling mindlessly in my hand.
I couldn't even finish saying the suras
before whispering aloud,
What am I supposed to do now?

HABITUAL PATTERNS

How many visits did it take?
One?
Three?
Six?
When did
Prayers then
Flowers then
Grave
Become a
Family tradition?
At what point
Did the
Urgency of
Death
Fade into the
Pattern of
Grief?
At what point
Did the tears
Dry into
Caked dirt,
Salt crystals
Caking streams
On face?
When did we
Become these
Creatures of habit?
How could time
Betray us.

HEADSTONE

On a random Thursday afternoon in the middle of July, Abbu forwarded a text message of a graphic without an explanation. In a black box it had Arabic text at the top. Under that it said "Makhfee S. Ahmed March 23, 1956 - June 02, 2011".

Please see proof for your review and approval, he texted right after.

Abbu's texts should come with a content warning. Each time he texts, it uncovers a well of trouble. We told him we didn't want a headstone — Ammu wouldn't have wanted one. But he went ahead anyways. Subordinate players to his grief.

I looked back at my phone then, pointedly remembering how a ukulele version of "Somewhere over the Rainbow" had been playing.

JASMINES

I brought her a single jasmine bud
from the bush in the garden
planted by her hands
hoping the night bloom
would fragrant her grave
with smells of home
the way she'd place
a small water bowl full of buds
on her nightstand
before she went to sleep
to fragrant her dreams.
She still sleeps,
her dreams now home.

Time Goes Fast

I accidentally bump into Abbu at the entrance of the graveyard
I am arriving and he is leaving, car windows roll down
Do you want me to go with you so we can pray together?

We stand at opposite sides of grave
Almost five years...? he mumbles, questioning.
It's been six years today, I respond firmly.

On his right hand, he counts on his fingers, in his village boy way
his thumb goes to the base of his pinkie finger
- 2011 -
he looks at the gravestone for confirmation
- 2012, 2013 -
thumb to each finger crease for each year
stopping in the middle of his ring finger.
He nods his head slowly, *six years* more to himself he says
a little louder, shocked, he says, *Time goes fast.*

Let's pray.
I raise my palms in supplication as tears drip down behind my sunglasses
listening to Abbu say Arabic words of suras I once knew but have
forgotten
thinking about how Time Goes Fast
and how he counted in his old-world way.

[ritual]

*The Quran and Sunnah indicate that the jinn
exist, and that there is a purpose for their
existence in this life, which is to worship Allah
Alone, with no partner or associate.*

*The jinn live on this earth where we do. They are
mostly to be found in ruins and unclean places
like bathrooms, dunghills, garbage dumps and
graveyards. Hence the Prophet (peace and
blessings of Allah be upon him) taught us to
take precautions when entering such places, by
reciting the adhkaar (prayers) prescribed by
Islam.*

Source: 'Belief in the Jinn', islamqa.info

JINN AT GRAVE

I thought I heard a jinn at the graveyard today.
As I stood silently graveside, I heard between the
rustling wind and over the sound of the distant
 little league game —the sound of Arabic prayers.
I thought my sister and I were alone at the grave.
Skipping over graves, walking tightrope on
concrete gravesite dividers, I follow the sound of
the mumbled duas, wondering if this was a pious
magical jinn that Muslim graves were known to reveal.
On the other side of the hedge behind the Sunni graveyard
 I see him, standing in front of a grave in the Shia section.
He was an older stout man, with a bushy mustache, reading
from a small leather book. I went back to my sister
and told her I had found a jinn in prayer,
don't you hear him? I asked.
Blasphemous, she whispered back.

As he walked by, holding two plastic grocery bags,
he said, *Salaams* as he passed us.
Wa alaykumu as-salam we responded in sync.
We waited a beat, then turned,
but we were alone at the grave again.
My sister saw him too,
that time, so I knew
it wasn't a dream.
Where did he go?
 my sister asked.
See? A jinn.
I replied.

Patriotic Puff Piece

I saw Ammu's grave
on the 10pm local news today
behind the white man
defending his right to
have American flags
waving on graves.

Cutaway, scene:
People running around graves
stabbing dirt with replacement flags
that had been accidentally thrown away.
A patriotic puff piece
for angry white people
on flags and patriotism.
Silly white people
and their puffy local news.

Cutaway, scene:
There in the far back,
there she was on my television.
There. She. Was.
On. My. TV.
Finally, in death,
she got her fifteen minutes of television fame.
Thank you, White Patriots—
but I couldn't help but notice
how you forgot to put a flag
at her grave, too.

TEARS BURIED IN THE GRAVEYARD OF MY CHEST

Of all the tears I can't cry
I feel these ones
buried at the feet of her grave the most.
My heart squeezes painfully
as I sit here where her toes should be.
Remember
where her head is,
direction faced towards Mecca,
and how I am here.
They say
paradise lies at the feet of your mother
but here is where I choke.
The graveyard of my chest
calloused with needle pricks
as the graveyard of her final resting place
grows weeds wildly out of control.

I sit and pull the weeds out frantically,
one at a time,
praying with each tug
wondering why the seeds I planted
eight years ago never rooted
and these did.
Maybe it is my lost tears
watering this soil now.
I almost cry when I see the family standing
at the newest grave
longing for when this grief was that unpracticed.

From nowhere, a train horn blows.
Overheard, a crow fights with a falcon
a breeze blows tickling my ankle
letting me know you are still here.
Did you take my tears with you when you left?
Do you take my tears with you every time you leave?

Haunting

Chapter 3

The Prophet Muhammad (pbuh) said,
"Your Heaven lies under the feet of your Mother."

IMPOSSIBLE EXISTENCE

How is it possible
that all that exists of you
are my memories?

PAST FOOTSTEPS FORWARD

At your mother's feet is the path to paradise
so I stood at the foot of her grave
and wondered how to step in, feet first.

Careful, pull out the weeds
paradise is not meant to be overgrown.
Where does the path of the feet of the childless go?

ECHOES EXISTING

 It is said that when people die
their life energy lingers
in the spaces where their body made the most impressions
— not ghost, not poltergeist, not exactly
more like echoes.
Life is cavernous
and bodies reverberate
calling back, long after it is gone.
At what point does it fade away fully?

WHEN THE WIND RUSTLES

Sometimes, it's a little thing. Like a rustling of a piece of paper, a curtain rattling the rod, a thing calling me over my shoulders.

I'll pause what I'm doing and turn to see what it is. There's usually nothing there. I'll cock my head to see if I can hear anything. Usually I'll hear nothing, except the wind.

I'll wonder if it's her, then. I'll sit quiet and try to feel with my intuition. I try hard to be still and empty my mind.

And then I stop. Not trusting my intuition because I can't feel her, I can't see her.

Maybe it was just the wind blowing, maybe that's all it ever was.

I pause. The world stops revolving for a brief second.

I don't know when she is here.

But I know when she is definitively not present.

And I wonder if I know one, how can I not know the other.

LAST TOUCH: FIRST TOUCH

I place my hand in the echoes of yours
your last touch shadows this space
on this perfume bottle
on this needlepoint
on this aerogram letter

They say
some paranormal spirits
are just the energy imprints
left behind when someone is gone

Is it like
two hands splayed together
with a glass window in-between

If my fingertips graze places yours have imprinted,
are you reaching back?

Can my first touch be your last touch in an otherworldly handhold?

In this impossible reality, can we be placed together again?

Cataract Surgery

The nurse asked, "Your blood pressure looks high, are you nervous?"
Abbu shook his head ever so slightly. Surprised, maybe. "It's fine. You
probably rushed here. It's just slightly high." She continued. "It says here
you are diabetic. Are you taking medication for that?" He looked at her,
blankly. After a few seconds, he shook his head. Muttered, "no."

"Borderline. You must be controlling with diet. Do you have a history of
diabetes?" I looked at him. I vaguely remember him saying something
about newly having diabetes. I didn't know the answer to that. He looked
confused. "My sisters, two, maybe three." he responded, after a while.

"He has 13 siblings, he's the youngest of fourteen." I said, explaining his
stutter. How are you supposed to remember the history of illness of so
many? How do you track hereditary? "Oh me, too. Big family. I'm one of
seven." She responded, her Tagalog tinged accent pronounced.

"Are you single or married?" she asked, continuing her pre-op checklist.
"Married," he responded, immediate. Confident. This he knew the
answer. "He's widowed," I corrected quietly staring at the floor, from my
side seat of the examination room. I peeked up at Abbu, sitting on the
ophthalmologist examination chair.

Behind his cataract-fogged eyes, I could see the wheels turn slowly in his
head. Was he translating the English term for widow to the Bangla?
 Did he forget, for a moment, and in his memory did she exist again? Just
that morning as I drove us to the hospital he had said, "Did I tell you
what happened? Last night, at the party one of the auntie's said,
'Bhabi khotay? Bhabi kay anou nay khenoh?' And then she covered her
mouth, and said, 'I'm sorry. I forgot.'"- Where is Bhabi? Why didn't you
bring her? - My eyes had welled immediately. Behind his cataract shaded
eyes, he couldn't tell. I said nothing...

"Widowed." He nodded his head slightly, in affirmation. In sadness? In
regret? His truth coming back to his reality. The nurse continued typing
on her keyboard, hardly glancing up. She missed the moment. Or maybe
she let us have it. "Okay, now, let's check your eye sight. Look up at the
wall right there. Tell me, what letters can you read?"

MY FACE IS HERS

They would say I had his face
his angry eyes
his furrowed brows
his stern jawlines.

I would cringe wanting rather
her sympathetic gaze
her sweet smile
her tender cheeks.

His face was full of rage
full of temper
love till the tipping point of mad.

In the mirror
I wondered if she could see me now inside out
but only my haunted eyes looked back.

COLD CREAM

I smell her before I feel her.
It is the scent of 80s cold cream,
like maybe Ponds or Nivea but stronger.
I look up from my book close my eyes inhale deep
yes, right, that's it
it is the scent from the violet-colored Avon jar
the creams that Ammu would always have on her dresser.
I open my eyes and look around,
alone in in her house
reading a book on the floor
of my childhood bedroom
breaking June gloom and distant sounds of freeway outside.
I smell my palms wondering if it could be me,
I try to read again, but the scent breezes by again
And I again, I wonder where the scent is coming from
I wonder if she is watching me.
I wonder what she sees.

ANNIVERSARY

1:35am
June 2nd
For the past 6 years
I've never been able to sleep
On this night
At this anniversary moment
With the memories of what I missed
Haunting my imagination —
Her voice shaken
She couldn't get out of bed
Sponge bath on patio
Refusal to go to the doctor
Walked herself to the car
Ambulance without the lights
IV drip that could have saved her
Failing organs
Code blue
Fingers in air moving
"I am praying"
Alone in the room
The sound of the flat line –
Haunting my imagination
Because I wasn't here to save her.
I wasn't here.

If time is relative and life is relative
I wonder if the afterlife has 365 days in a year
Or is this time-pass irrelevant
What is a 'death anniversary'
But just another moment of faded memory
365 times 6 times 24 over
If you ask me what's happened in the past six years
Nothing. It feels like nothing.
Time passed irrelevant.

MEMORIAL DAY

If I could time machine back six years to this very day
I would whisper to myself, *do not hang up the phone*
Tell her tell her tell her
Tell her we will be okay
Tell her not to be scared
Tell her she is loved
Tell her we will figure life out
Tell her again, to go to the doctor
Tell her to fight for her life but let her know we forgive her if she doesn't
Tell her that you will pray for her
Tell her that Nana will join her soon
Tell her about the dream about her and the rattlesnake
Tell her to visit you in your dreams
Tell her we need her but we understand if she can't stay
Tell her you are sorry, for everything, and that you love her.
Tell her not to worry, the angels will hold her
Tell her you miss her now and you will always...

TRANSLATION TECHNOLOGY

I ask the app, *Is this goat, beef, or mutton?* He translates, in the warm voice of an older Bengali man, *Eeh chahgual, ghuru mankhshou, bah mahtin?* His voice is only slightly tingy, filtered across time and modern technology. Next time, I will ask at Deshi to the Bengali uncle behind the counter, first practicing how to say this in my car before walking in, then casually asking if that dish in the buffet right there, *Eeh chahgual, ghuru manshou, bah mahtin?* He is never rude, but his side-eye on my incomplete Bangla makes me feel a kind of way. I just want to know what I am eating.

I ask the app, *Is there salt in the water?* And I know by the *lohbhan* and *pani* that this app was translated for people Bangladeshis like me.

I then ask the app to translate, *You are very pretty, you are gorgeous, you did very well today, I am so proud of you, You are so smart, You are a success, Did I mention how proud I am of you? Don't let the world get you down — you are deserving, I love you.* I am comforted by the familiarity of the Bangla words, words I haven't heard since I was little — these are words that I once recognized from back in time. And though it is the voice of an older man, I can hear my mother's voice in it. And I hear my Nani's voice. And I hear my Nana's voice. Their voices of when they are younger, and when I was child and affirmations flowed free-er. And I play it again, grasping at a long past nostalgia that I no longer have the language for.

THE PAGES OF HER SONG BOOK

I.

Tattered edge song book
Sits idle in a mother tongue
No longer mine.

II.

Harmoniously
Over harmonium breath
Tagore brought to life.

III.

Lyricized pages
Fall like blue-inked paper rain,
Earth bound no longer.

WHO HOLDS THESE IMAGES

Sifting through small black and white photos
of memories that weren't mine
from a palace that no longer exists.
tell me a story of why her brows furrowed here
when Nani made her wear a sari
how her voice vibrato-ed while playing the harmonium
the way you took breakfast in the garden during winters
where would the trains take you across South Asia
why was she riding a horse if she was scared of them
And when you had to flee Lahore to Bangladesh
with nothing but what you could carry
how did these photos survive all the way to Los Angeles?
Now, in this dusty shoebox of a memory palace.
What do I do with them, now.

UNRAVELING

I spent last night before Mother's Day
sifting through Ammu's old jewelry boxes
looking for a locket.
I caressed the dusty rings all lined up in velvet
fingers sieved through cheap plastic earrings
jhumkas jangled with each tug of a box.

"What do you want me to find?" I asked
out loud to the stagnant room
as I went through one box after another
unzipping tanned leather boxes with red suede interior
unclasping flat red velour containers
opening tiny oak drawers

I found the strings of Bangladeshi pink pearls
filigree of bright 14k gold
plastic and enamel geometric shaped earrings
and holiday themed Avon cosmetic jewelry.
She wore these chandelier earrings with that rose sari
or that enamel pin on her red work vest
these rings she stopped wearing when her fingers got too fat
those pieces she was saving for a special dawat
this "Mom" charm I got her for her last Mother's Day
that she ended up never wearing at all.
I took a little bit of solace that her spirit
could be lingering in these gems
maybe I shouldn't cleanse them after all
a time travel touch through jewelry

Ammu had told the Medium she wanted me to wear
the locket she used to always wear,
to be held close to my heart chakra
but all I had was her old gold chain tied together with string.
"Show me where to look," I asked
sitting on the floor, every corner unturned
there is nothing left to find.

I wondered if maybe
it was part of the set of gold that she had pawned off in the end
I don't even know what I'm looking for
but I know I haven't found it yet.

LONGING IN AEROGRAMS

On the single pale blue thin paper of
the carefully opened aerogram letter
longing was caught in the space between.
Slanted blue ink tiny script splayed across the page
but along the creases and empty margins
did the immigrant longing reside.
It rested in the mundane sentences
of the latest seventies' dreamy TV hero
in the exclamations of boredom
at starting school again
in the simplicity of mentioning
who was getting married to whom
who was leaving the country next.
Longing existed in the spaces between,
"Tell us who is your baby's personality like?"
"What is your husband all about?"
"How do you spend your days?"
"How come we haven't heard from you?"
"Why don't you call anymore?"
There's never an
I miss you —
I love you —
come back to us –
that's implied
in the margins/ space/ blankness.
But you can't send a letter of emptiness.
In Ammu's closet in a dusty box to the back
we found these stacks of
blue aerogram letters sent
from Bangladesh
from her parents and sisters
from the 80s
two decades of letters from three decades ago.
A box full of longing in the empty margins.
and now she is gone
being longed for once again.

[ritual]

When the wings of the night spread - or when evening comes - keep your children in, for the devils come out at that time. Then when part of the night has passed, let them go. And close the doors and mention the name of Allah, for the shaytaan does not open a closed door. And tie up your water skins and mention the name of Allah, and cover your vessels and mention the name of Allah, even if you only put something over them, and extinguish your lamps.

Source: 'When the wings of the night spread, keep your children in, for the devils come out at that time', islamqa.info

SUNSETS

Let me tell you about sunsets
about Maghreb
about calling us back home.
Let me tell you about swooping jinns, green flashes and tickled toes.
Let me tell you about the pink tubes of acrylic
about blending gradients
about painting echoes.
Let me tell you how colored canvass hug me home.

They say
if you look at setting sun over the ocean
you will see a green flash of light precisely
as the last piece of sun sinks on the horizon.
I can't tell you how many times
I've stared at the horizon
trying to capture green rays through squinted eyes.
They also say
if you are a woman with uncovered hair out at Maghreb time
jinns will swoop down and grab you by the hair.
I can't tell you how many times
I've stared at the dimming sky
wondering if that gendered fear tactic
really worked.

Sunsets in Oakland are bright
with shocking ruby reds
streaks of orange.
Sometimes violet speckles the skyline.
Colors so bright they are violent
tearing through the sky and
ripping clouds in colors.

Sunsets in Southern California,
on the other hand
are muted and dusky.
It's the brisk desert chill or
the cloudless bitter skies

making the Instagram-ed awning look
like a flashback to the 70s.
The pale pinks
fade into pale blues
into lightly dusted stars.
When it's Maghreb time
it's almost like there is an exhale
a relief to the hot sands and palms
as the night chill descends.
The mountains shadows in lavender
 and palms fronds silhouette the cloudless graying ceiling.

How does one capture this with paint?
I've collected tubes of magenta, fuchsia and cadmium
with failed attempts of just that.
My canvasses are a manic array of California sunset rays
pinks streak, blues fade and stars dance.
But there are no colors for the sweeping jinns
for the almost green flash
for azaans calls to prayer
or for ghosts tickling toes.

How do you paint the quieting drone of rush hour traffic ending
or the chirps of a hummingbird suckling on Mexican sage?
How do you paint Santa Ana winds combing through palm fronds
or Ammu's voice calling you inside for prayer?

It's the sounds of sunsetting that make me nostalgic for home
nostalgia of sitting on the carpet in my childhood bedroom
daydreaming out the window
and listening to the silent descend.
Waiting for Ammu's voice
calling me to prayer.
And calling me home.
It's the hum of what's missing
that I hear in those colors.

How do you paint that?

HEALING

CHAPTER 4

" Ya Allah, let this day ahead of us and every tomorrow
that we see, be filled with openings to grow in our
character by living goodness and give us the wisdom to
seize those openings in every good way possible. Protect
us always from hearts that are not humble, tongues that
are not wise and eyes that have forgotten how to cry.
Forgive us for our shortcomings and guide and bless us
all. Ameen."

- Imam Khalid Latif

Mother's Fallow Garden

On the anniversary of the last time we spoke
I dug my fingers into the very dirt
that likely killed her.
Snapdragons and marigolds and azaleas and petunias.
Remember how colorful these gardens were
the morning after her death –
bright and lush like the blooms hadn't heard the news yet.
Without her hands over all these years, the soil has run fallow.
How could the people living in this house not realize
the importance of keeping her garden alive ... when she wasn't.
Even though I was hungry
I fed the plant roots with soil and nourished their growth.
Even though I was parched
I watered the ground till the plants would thirst for no more.
Even after all these years.
The sadaqah from planting these seeds just a fraction
of what she received from her lifetime of nurturing living things.
It wasn't until I was in the shower
cleaning the dirt from under my nails
did I realize what I had done on what day it was.
I will never forget how her voice quivered that day
as she told me over the cackling line of the phone
that she had spent Memorial Day weekend
gardening and that her body felt
strange because of it.
I am still fasting.

SEVEN YEARS

Seven-year itch
with copper or wool
or weeding dandelions at graves.
Has too much time passed to cry?
I'll still buy you flowers for this day.
Countdown to death
count back after till death will us part
a seven-year generation gap.

CRY IF I WANT TO

Make me cry.

Tears were buried in the
depth of the graveyard in my sternum
energetic block was breaking my heart
but I didn't cry.
I couldn't.

Tears were not shed at the grave,
or grasping crystals or counting thosbees,
or when Ammu sent messages from beyond
or when needles were stuck into the place it hurt
or listening to heart-achy ballads
or when the man didn't kiss me back
or the jinn danced circles of fires on my back.
I lost my cry.

The pain pierces concaving within itself
my hand rests in my cleavage
holding it in place
five times a day
no tears, for fear.
I'd forgotten how to cry.

Where have my tears buried within themselves
When did I become so numb?
If crying is my medical prescription,
 where will this pain go
if I can't make me cry, again?

PAPER THIN SKIN

It was tiny
the size and shape of a dime
with the thinness of rice paper,
flesh toned of a White person and
stick like a band aid.
My task was to find
a clean spot on his upper arm
to attach a fresh patch nightly
after dinner of the maach and dhal and bhaath,
and Maghreb prayer under the monsoon clouds,
and his 100 scuffled exercise steps with the bamboo cane,
and the nightly read out loud because he could no longer read.
After the cocktail of three pills and eight eye drops.

His skin was so paper thin,
mottled with brown age spots, fade spots
and graying hair.
Look at my skin, touch it. I think something's wrong with it.
Why does it feel like this?
The skin sagged in the way it does
when muscles disappear
and atrophy sets in.
So thin his skin
that I squirmed afraid
nervous a piece would rip right off
and it did
as his arm showed dime scars
of rips from before
spotted scars on mottled skin.

The patch was the medicine that kept Nani lurking in his shadows
and Ammu a daughter in his dreams.
It was the thing
that kept the hallucination of the burglars to just whispers
and the raucous living room party
to just a figment of his imagination.

For eleven days
it was just us two,
Nathni and Nana,
Granddaughter and grandfather,
caregiver and care taken,
petering around that huge mansion in Kathmandu
haunted with the ghosts that we brought with us from around the world
—

me, haunted by the dreams and memories
and he, haunted by the memories he was unable to remember.

Feed him, nap him and medicate him
but they had warned me
it wouldn't be easy.
Nothing could have prepared me
for the dementia he paced in.
It's a crazy thing to see someone go crazy.
Enough to make one disillusioned.

Every night
as my nails carefully lifted the patch off his skin
ripping my own circle scars into my Nana's paper skin
I toyed with the idea of skipping this patch
so he could see the shadows crawling on his skin
make sense of the flickering lights
so he could speak to them.
Would Nani emerge from the shadows
Would he be able to caress her?
Would Ammu walk in from the dreams?
Would he be able to hug her?
Talk to her?
Could he tell her he loved her?
And then maybe, just maybe,
he could tell me?

My aunt told me before she left
that the angels had paid him a visit
on his last battle with death.
They told him it wasn't his time.
He was sent back

to the dementia medicated dream
where reality and pretend and dreams and memories blurred
the limbo between nap time and prayer time
the space between the sajda and the floor
Bata slippers and wooden canes as accessories
and handkerchiefs tucked in knots of checkered lungis
Grandfather sweaters
And watches hidden under pillows
And prayer rugs folded with thopis
and yellowed turmeric stained finger nails
and that paper skin
falling away and apart.
Fragile body wrapped precariously
in that transparent shadow crawling
rice paper thin
transparent paper skin.

I didn't.
But every night I wondered what would happen if I did.
And that maybe his dementia world was more real
than this paper thin reality could ever be.

DISPOSABLE FIRE

Hold it still, I said stern
as the sparkler stick shook
in tiny clenched fists

I want to do it! she squealed
her child eyes lit with fear and excitement
and giddy anticipation
memory of last year so far
it was like a new memory all over

Lighter clicked
Hold it far from your face
Flame caught
clenched fist turned into pyro glow sticks
glowing neon green magic
glinted off her big brown eyes
as she went running
joining her sister
both twirling
in the middle of the dark street
littered with paper embers
singed to the pavement
Paratroopers. Starburst. Whistler.

Smoke danced a trail behind them
stinging my eyes and
filling my mouth with
the acrid taste of a hot California summer night

Be careful! I screamed down the street
The ever always big sister
A few blocks over
explosion cracks through the silence
We all look up
synchronized
to see red flames fountain over rooftops in the sky

This was back when it was easy
back before city bans
and surreptitious purchases one town over
This was when Roman candles
could be bought from roadside wooden shacks
like sweet summer strawberries
Back when Muslim teens could buy explosives
without getting carded

Ammu liked the ones that would
whirl close to the ground
like a swirling dervish dancer
wheezing in delight

She'd sit heavy
lawn chair in driveway
her brood running in between flames with
sparklers in fists
She'd clap her swollen hands with that childlike innocence
her meaty arms close by her side
Her eyes would be lit up
Big smile on her face

She always had that childlike innocence to her, even as an adult,
Her best friend would tell me years later
as we stood by Ammu's freshly filled grave

But this was back before
And from her folding chair throne
Ammu was the inelegant queen
never telling us to step back
Or that we'd burn ourselves
or lose an arm
Redundant, I guess
From her chair she yelled out,
Do it again, do it again!
Clapping

I had seen enough late-night news clips
to know it could all go terribly awry

Don't touch it! I'd scold
Sisters suddenly jumping back, giggling
as I bent down to light each disposable canister
placed gently in the middle of the street
and then RUN
back to the driveway
heart in throat.
Fire starts jumping
and squealing in pain
Red, squeal.
Green, poppopopop.
White, crackle.

Mesmerized
we all stood by Ammu's side
muted
neon lights reflecting all of our smoke tinged eyes
flames blistering wildly on the street
till the explosions extinguished
sputtering into silence

One more time! Again!

That was the last one. There's no more.

Quietly we stood
smoke heavy in air
disposable fireworks extinguished

There's no more.
There's no more.

Khala's Iftar

Prophet Muhammad (pbuh) said, "There is none amongst the Muslims who plants a tree or sows seeds, and then a bird, or a person or an animal eats from it, but is regarded as a charitable gift for him."

**

Have some, my Khala said, somberly, pushing the Tupperware of green colored beans coated in turmeric. *This was your Ammu's favorite food – sheem. I grew it in my garden. Khao.*

> *I still miss her,* my aunt's subtext said, somberly. *I love you because you are a piece of her. I nurtured her memory to never forget.*

I ate it, wordlessly, despite it not being my favorite food.

Take some home in this plastic yogurt container. Don't protest. Chee.

> *This is how I show I love you, still. Do you still love me?*

I took it home, quietly, despite knowing it would just sit in my fridge.

Who gets the credit sadaqah from eating the food grown from Khala's seed in my mother's memory?

> We broke our fast tonight, but this fast will last a lifetime.

> We've already been fasting for almost eight years.

YOGURT CONTAINERS

You will forget what it held
but will remember how the contents held you
the 32-ounce plastic yogurt containers
as old as time
tested, tried and true
nested, white and blue
holding memories
a container of nostalgia stains
yellowed from years of turmeric and wordless love
and never leaving another's home empty-handed.
Don't be rude.
How many times this plastic passed hands
time travel through the kitchen cabinet of empty plastics
the magic of opening a yogurt container in the refrigerator
and finding it is never yogurt inside it.

ABBU TRIED

Remember when I worked there? Abbu pointed to the truck stop.

I remember when someone died while you worked there, I said offhand, as I kept driving us by.

I tried to save her life, he responded quietly.

He said that the woman was lying on the train tracks, was probably drunk. She had been a driver in a semi-truck and they had parked at the truck stop. He said when he saw her, she was already lying on the tracks with her head really close to a rail. She was knocked out, either passed out from alcohol or knocked by a previous train. He ran out from his booth when he saw her, and saw that there was another train coming down the tracks. He said he grabbed her arm and tried to pull her off the tracks. He could see the train coming and knew the train wouldn't see her in time to stop. He pulled her, but she wasn't moving. But he was able to move her head off the track just in time. When he saw she was safe, he ran inside and called 911. But by the time the police arrived, they were too late.

But he didn't know that. Not until a few days later when the police came back to the stop and told him she was dead.

You're a hero, my sister said from the backseat. *I never heard of this story before.*

"But he didn't save her life, I said.

But at least he tried, my sister replied. *He's a hero for trying.*

TIME PASS INTO THE PAST

Pause in the mirror and wonder who you see.
You are unrecognizable but everything is seen.
Those under eye bags look like your Nani's
and that age spot is where your father's is.
When did your mother's jowls creep onto your face?
Touch your finger to where wrinkles creep in under eye cream
push cheeks to see how the collagen has left
Has that blue vein always been visible there?
Look at how the scar from where you hit your head as a toddler
or the burn marks on the back of your 6yr old hand and
how they have faded.
You had always wondered how your scars
would show up under aged skin.
Spend hours staring at yourself in the mirror and
wonder if you'll ever recognize
yourself ever again.

GIGGLES AT GRAVES

We laughed all the way to grave. Because it was too tiring to be somber all the time. It started with a smirk at the place we prayed. It turned into a contagious giggle as we got into the car. Before we knew it, everyone in the car was uproariously laughing. People were giggling even though they didn't hear the joke and they didn't know why. That's how contagious of a mirth it was. Strangers told us how beautiful we looked. That's how apparent our joy was. We wondered, silently, to ourselves, if our laughter was brazen. We thought, in our minds, if people who looked like us were dying, if the world was so tragic, that our laughter was callous. Cavalier, even.

But we couldn't help ourselves. It was like big belly bursting at the seams – the stress of it, everything in living, made us all feel so much. If we couldn't laugh, we'd have to cry, but our tears were exhausted from sadness. So all we had left to do was laugh.

At the graveyard we smiled as we skipped over gravestones. We quietly chuckled as we placed flowers on our mother's grave. Our recited duas were whispered through smiling lips. We looked at the mourners crying at the new graves, recent in death, freshly grieving. Was that longing that rumbled in our hearts? Was it possible that we missed the feeling of sadness? We looked on to them with clear eyes, wondering how heartless we were for not feeling that gut-wrenching pain anymore. Guilty for our happiness, we avoided eye contact in the guise of giving the grievers room to grieve. We wanted to tell them, in time, they would remember how to laugh again, too. We wanted to tell them that when healing from grief, they must remember how to laugh. We wanted to tell them grief would be constant so their joy must be louder.

We drove away from the graveyard, crying only tears of laughter. Till we could laugh no more.

NOTES

Many of the poems found in this collection were written in conjunction with published essays also on the theme of grief.

Radical Love monthly column, oveinshallah.com 2012-2015
'The Cost of Grief 'in *Good Girls Marry Doctors*, 2016
'Patches' in *Modern Loss*, 2018
'Intimidating' in *Pretty Bitches*, 2020

ABOUT THE AUTHOR

Tanzila "Taz" Ahmed is a political strategist, storyteller, and artist based in Los Angeles. She creates at the intersection of counternarratives and culture-shifting as a South Asian American Muslim 2nd-gen woman. Her essays are published in the anthologies Pretty Bitches, Whiter, Good Girls Marry Doctors, Love Inshallah, and numerous online publications. In Spring 2019 she was UCLA's Activist-in-Residence at the Institute on Inequality and Democracy, and in 2016, she received an award from President Obama's White House as a Champion of Change in Art and Storytelling.

Made in the USA
Columbia, SC
04 July 2023